My Dad (Mr. P)

THE POET AND HE DIDN'T KNOW IT

My Dad (Mr. P)

THE POET AND HE DIDN'T KNOW IT

Steve Piranio

ARPress

ARPress
45 Dan Road Suite 5
Canton MA 02021
Hotline: 1(888) 821-0229
Fax: 1(508) 545-7580

Ordering Information:

Quantity sales. Special discounts are available on quantity purchases by corporations, associations, and others. For details, contact the publisher at the address above.

Printed in the United States of America.

ISBN-13:   Softcover   979-8-89356-065-7

                  eBook   979-8-89356-066-4

Library of Congress Control Number: 2024903755

Special thanks to Paula Warner, the artist for the book, in Ord NE, Elizabeth Johnson, the notary, in Hastings, NE

Before my life is done
I would like to have a hole in one

But if you would see my stroke
You might say, "Ain't that a joke"

I hit the ball in a trap full of sand
When no one was looking, I throw out by hand

My next shot was on the green, close to the hole
Made my putt and missed, I could have kicked it in with my toe

Gentleman said, "Do you want to play another round"
I thought to myself, his mind is not very sound

Another round I thought I would play
Got to get better, but not today.

Did I run so fast I could not see
the thing that people call me

As I let the time slip by
I miss the thing called I

Most of my life seems to be gone
I have missed me and that is wrong

The mirror must be too dirty to see
the thing I missed was seeing me.

Would there be a night
　　"Without you"
Dinner by candlelight
　　"Without You"
Will there be days fishing
　　"Without You"
Or days just wishing
　　"Without You"
Will there be walks in the park
　　"Without You"
Is there cuddling in the dark
　　"Without You"
Life must go on
　　"But not without you"

Lost Along The Way

May be I got lost along the way
Wish there were things I could change today

Might take a while for people to cool
You might call me weak by another man's rule

This may not have been the time for our paths to cross
Whether it's you or me, this can be a loss

My poems and roses are what I sent
I thought this is what God had meant.

The Lineman

We put on our spikes and climb to the top
The lines are down, the power has stopped

Listen to the wires how they hum
Work smart, be careful, don't work dumb

Ice and snow, another big storm
We have to work to keep warm

Here is the crew, all huddled together
Hoping for a break in the weather

We must climb although it's cold
Sometimes I think I'm getting old

Can I sit and watch a rose grow
Or wait for its beauty after the snow
Just to see so much beauty unfold
For a rose is the prettiest flower I am told
A garden or roses for everyone to see
A rose for you and a rose for me
To have a garden where it grows
Is to know the beauty of a rose
A vase of roses on the mantle or one on a shelf
For every rose has a story in itself

Little Sister Liz

My Little Sister Liz,
Our time is here.
God's picture is very clear.
Here on earth we leave all that is dear.

Unselfishly you gave your love.
It will be returned to you on the wings of a dove.
God's face is for you to see
Pray for us and save a place for me.

Love,
Your Brother Joe

As the wind blows from east to west

You are the gentle breeze, that puts me to rest

If I traveled the seas and sky so blue

Through all my travels it should be with you

Lift me to the top and take me to the heights

Whatever you do, keep me in sight

My life may not be full of riches and fame

To have you, I'll be the person you tame

I know my life has not been great

You are a lady and you're first rate

So to you, Carol, I would like to say

Let's spend more time than just a day

When a relationship loses its taste,
To go on would be a waste.

If you no longer see eye to eye,
That should be the time to say goodbye.

Things you saw, are no longer there.
It's now because two people do not care.

The test of love, together problems they share.
For if one says nothing, the other should beware.

The test of time was all we had.
To lose time and love, that's very sad.

To say together would be a crime.
All we would do is waste each other's time.

To say goodbye is what we must do.
To give you a chance to find someone new.

Whoever he is, I hope he is true.
And, all the happiness he'll give to you.

My Mother

Mom, We know you are gone
Life is just for a while.
You will be missed.
You taught your children to smile.
God has taken you to a heaven so blue
He has a place and it's just for you.

Your fears, loneliness, and sorrows
Are no longer here.
I know you are in heaven
With souls so dear.

Mom, all we can do for you
Is to pray
Because I know we will be
With you some day.

Your son,
Joseph

Miracle

Had a miracle in my hand
Not knowing or able to understand

To you Lord I do pray
Please return the miracle some day

Change my life so I could see
The wonderful thing you had for me

I look to you and the heaven above
For what I lost was more than love

Lost the something that was true
The sky so dark when it was once blue

I do not pray in haste
Lost a miracle that's a waste

I hope the miracle would return again
With God's help I'll know how to begin.

I lost that shining star
When I reached it was too far

As I see the star in the heaven above
Is there not one that I could love

There! There is my star, shining so bright
The sun appears, it loses its light

I will someday find my star
When I reach it will not be too far

If I had my life to live over again
Where would I start?
How would I begin?
Would I have the dreams I had before?
Or would there be no dreams anymore?
Would I live to be strong and bold?
And could I live to be gray and old?

Upon The Hill

I saw a cross upon a hill
A body nailed and very still,
And down below a mother weeps
Not knowing her son only sleeps
For like the sun, he too shall rise
In hopes to save all our lives.

Love was here, now it's gone
It seems to be something we can't keep long

I have prayed from day to day
Will this love I have stay?

The only thing I could be is me
This is what the other does not see

The life I lived may be too long
Only to have love and not keep it strong

If life goes on without you
There are things we should do

The hardest thing in life is to say goodbye
To those that live or those that die

A Home

A home is for two
A house just for you.

Peace of mind
Is for us to find.

If the truth cannot be
Then there is no place for you and me.

Clouds Go By

As I sit and watch the clouds go by
I sit and wonder who and why
Wondering what makes a tree grow.
Why must it die in the snow?
There a garden of roses, pale in the moonlight
Then the sun comes out, they seem so bright.
Thunder and lightning and then the rain
Roses and trees begin to grow again.
Who put all this here for us to see
Whoever he is, he's bigger than me.

Nancy, watch the clouds and listen to the rain.
    He, who is bigger than us, will make it happen again.

Thanks for letting me know you.

Mistakes

One day when I awake
I will wonder who made the mistake.

Was it you…or was it me?
Or was it things we could not see.

I had a chance to see the Easter Bunny
He left Easter eggs, but no money.

I asked him if he was hungry and would like to eat
He thanked me and said he had other children to meet.

Why does Easter come only once a year?
He was so nice and such a dear.

He could live with me and we'd have fun
He could hop, and I could run.

I would have the Easter Bunny, and that would be nice
But I would let him see other children at least once or twice.

To my lovely wife on Valentine's day,
I want to take the time to say...
Thank you for the wonderful years.
Through it all, we shared our tears.
Life with you has been grand!
Your love is what I understand.
All the years we've shared our time
Won't you be my valentine.

Three Kings looked from town to town

To see where the newborn babe could be found

As the star shines so bright

It led the Kings through the night

As they traveled with gifts of myrrh, incense and gold

for the Savior is born, they were told

When we met, we had a dream
Guess it was not what it seems

What did I have to offer you
After your life, nothing new

Could not be like your other men
To me that was my only sin

We were to be honest with one another
That we couldn't be to each other

It took me awhile to realize
Why you can't look me in the eyes

What did you expect to see
When you looked at me.

Christmas Time Again

Oh, to be a child once more
To see Christmas toys on the floor
And look under the Christmas tree
All the good things for you and me.

If, in my life, one day I could choose,
Christmas would be the day I would never loose.
As our life goes on, we grow old
Christmas stories to our children are told.
The children are happy, for Santa is near
Then all awaken to see Santa and his reindeer.
To all of you peace and happiness for more than a year.

So from me, a Merry Christmas and a happy new year.

Who Am I

I must find out who I am
    is this the me of the "I" that can talk
                "I" that can hear
                "I" that can smell
                "I" that can see
                "I" that can touch

I must find the I so to find the me of me
    then I will know the "I" that can listen
                "I" that can understand
                "I" that can feel
                "I" that can care
                "I" that can share

then I'll know that me of me and I will be the "I that can Love" Hope you like this, always keep a remember me.

Here is the dad for the kids
Grandpa send it for X-mas

Your grandpa
Love, Dad

Mary Queen of Love

Send peace and happiness from above
Please give help to those in need
Hoping some would return your deed

The Rosary you gave to us to pray
Hoping it's done each and every day
Beautiful roses you gave to us
To show us your love and trust

Mother of the world and all its love
Your beauty, trust and love, your sign, the white dove

He Walked With Me

As I sat and looked out to sea
I saw a man walking toward me.

As we sat for a delicious feast
He assured me I was not one of the least.

As we walked all over this land
We walked, but he led me by the hand.

He showed me all the pain and sorrow
And said we must pray for a better tomorrow,

When he showed me the nails so deep
I wondered why the world didn't weep.

If we had love
    But we missed
Whatever the reason
    We could make a list
When there Is love
    And it doesn't last
There must be no regrets
    So put in the past
For when we love
    We give of ourselves

If I can find my life's worth,

It would be time well spent on earth.

My worth would not be that of silver or gold,

But someone to love, someone to hold.

Things of value, they soon pass.

True love will always last.

Time together in love, is time well spent.

For this is what God has sent.

We're here on earth our shortest time,

So please won't you be my Valentine.

Christmas comes but once a year,
A time for happiness and good cheer.
Our Christmas tree with lights so bright,
Children staying up half the night.
The children are playful and very gay,
For Santa will be here today.
A Christmas with snow so bright,
Children on their sleigh, such a delight.
No presents of diamonds or gold,
A gift of love and someone to hold.

Merry Christmas

A Child Again

Oh, to be a child once more,
To see Christmas toys on the floor,
And look under the Christmas tree,
All the good things for you and me.

If, in my life, one day I could choose
Christmas would be the day I would never lose.
As life goes on, we grow old,
Christmas stories to our children are told.
The children are happy, for Santa is near.
They're all awake to see Santa and his reindeer.

Peace and happiness to you for
More than a year,
So from me
Merry Christmas and a Happy New Year!

The miracle of life is birth
For this is what we give the earth

We give each other a son of new life
Guide and teach and give him strength through his strife

For each of you have something to give
To build his mind, body, and love to live

His first teachers will be the two of you
Give him love of life, he will always be true.

Joe and Carol

The Passover

Moses and his people wandered for 40 years

He took them from slavery and fear,

Matzo from heaven was their food

A miracle they never understood,

Ten commandments I give to you

Follow them…a god will be true

Through the war, death they gave

God sent them love, so he can save.

Then he gave them a promised land

He gave them love and strength to walk hand in hand.

One day when the world is new

I will thank god I was born a Jew.

The land, mountains, and the sea
God created them just for me

As I sit in the forest and look at the trees
I sit quietly and listen to the breeze

Look at the mountains, so large and tall
God put them there, so we know we are small

Sitting and looking out to the sea
Why, God, can I not see me?

Let Us Smile

Sometimes life can be very rough
Someone at your side may be enough,

There will come a time, help we might need
If help you get, please return the deed,

Open your heart. there are things to do
For the good you do will be returned to you,

If I hurt you or brought you sorrow
Please forgive me. we hope for a better tomorrow,

When we see each other, let us smile
For we are only here for a short while.

If we can't help each other
Let's not hurt one another.

Alone

As I sit alone and grow old
I wonder what stories would be told.

Sitting and staring into space
How many old are in my same place?

We can sit alone and wonder and pray
Will our loneliness be gone today?

To be with people to love and enjoy
Happiness like a child with a new toy.

I know some day my life god will take
I hoped and prayed mine was no mistake.

Hear My Prayer

I hope he hears me pray
Does he not know the feeling in me,
The things I need. He surely can see
In my loneliness from day to day
To give me happiness and a cheerful way,
Help me be good instead of being bad
To make people happy instead of sad.
Clear my mind and make it your tool
Give me the goodness to keep your rule.

The World Today

What is happening in the world today?
There are things we can do and do what we say.

Look at the things that are in our life.
It is sad when you hear of a battered wife.

An abused child is so bad to see,
Be thankful it has not happened to you or to me.

Men and women in prison for crimes they commit.
When they return to society, Will they fit?

People are together and yet they must hide.
They have low self-esteem and very little pride.

Let's work together and pitch in.
There must be ways to stop this sin.

There are things we can do to help.
We must find the way.
If you need help, be not afraid to ask.

Do it today.

My Children

As I sit and watch my children play
I think how many times will I have this day.
As they grow tall, strong, and bold
Will they sit and watch dad grow old.

Will we have things we can savor
And I keep the memories of them forever,
For my children have been a wonderful thing of joy
they will be loved forever whether girl or boy,

If there is only one or two or even five,
Keep their memories happy and alive
For when I pass and leave this land
May they always remember me and walk hand in hand,

I am a proud man, as you can see by far
May be poor, but successful, because of what they are
May they have love, happiness, and peace
For this an eternity, I can rest in peace.

To see a bride on her wedding day,
a thing of beauty in every way

As she's walking down the aisle,
a beautiful lady with a wondrous smile.

Life together they must share,
happiness together to show they care.

As time goes on, and the years have passed,
only truth and honesty will make it last.

It's not important where the wedding must be,
but their love together, each other they see.

Looking Back

The wind will always blow
Roses and trees will always grow

Forests with a green hue
Grass glistening under the dew

Beauty that we seldom see
It was put here for you and me

Why can't we see the things that are here
Moving so fast we miss all that is near

We missed our children they grew so fast
When we are older we look to what has passed

We are now in our last stage
Hoping to have more knowledge because of age

The time will come when we must depart
So my friends hold me dear to your heart.

Just above my head where I can't see
is my guardian angel watching over me

You have your angel, I have mine
our only wish is to see our angel in time

She guides me from wrong to right
and she watches me each and every night

Through God's hand, I was given one
my angel will be with me till my time is done

Look At Me

We have eyes to look and see
Please let her eyes turn to look at me.
As you can see, she is the top
But in her eyes, I have been a flop.

If all the dates she had made with me
If they were kept, how happy we would be
For all the things that we have done in hopes to please
To gain her respect and love, would put me at ease.

To hold, to touch, to love her is such a delight
Without her beside me makes a long night.
Some day she will know me and understand
And this day forever we will walk hand in hand.

Here is a lady with a voice lovely and light,
In her arms I love to hear a good night.
When I'm with her, I value her time,
But I do wish more were mine.
There are doubts, loneliness, and fears.
In her arms we could share the tears.
Sometimes we may not be together,
But what I have of her, I have forever

I came this way
But not to stay
For I too shall have a day.

And when I'm gone
Remember me long
When I'm laid to rest
May it read "I've done my best."

In Loving Memory Of
JOSEPH L. PIRANIO

Born January 17, 1931
Died July 9, 2010
Age 79 Years

Looking Back

The wind will always blow
Roses and trees will always grow
Forests witha a green hue
Grass glistening under the dew
Beauty that we seldom see
It was put here for you and me
Why can't we see the things that are here
Moving so fast we miss all that is near
We missed our children they grew so fast
When we are older we look to what has passed
We are now in our last stage
Hoping to have more knowledge because of age
The time will come when we must depart
So my friends hold me dear to your heart

by Joe Piranio

Passantino Bros. Funeral Home

About the Author

Joseph L. Piranio is kind, loving, and a sincere person who loves his family. He always puts other people first. He can put a smile on anyone's face. He would start a conversation with anyone. As for hobbies, he has lots. He would go fishing and race pigeons. His favorite one was singing Frank Sinatra's song, "My Way!" in karaoke sessions. His on-circuit name was Mr. P. Everyone knew him as that. He was a U.S. Navy veteran. He served in the Korean War. He worked as an electrician for Kansas City. He helped build projects like Worlds of Fun, the Kansas City International Airport, and Liberty Hospital. He has five grandchildren and four great-grandchildren. One of the things he is great at was writing down his thoughts as poems. He would teach his two sons to hunt and fish. Anyone who knows him knows family is very important to him in every way.